Vending Machine Business Startup For Beginners 2022

The Complete Guide on How to Start, Grow and Promote a Profitable Vending Machine Business.

Howard J. Wall

Copyright © 2022 by Howard J. Wall- All rights reserved.

No part of this publication may be reproduced, stored in a retrieval system or transmitted in any form or by any means, electronic, mechanical, photocopying, recording, and scanning without permission in writing by the author.

Contents

Introduction 1

Chapter 1 5

How to Start a Vending Machine Business 5

    The Benefits of Owning a Vending Machine Business 6

    How to start from the Ground Up 9

    Find out where the machines are and sign contracts. 11

    Increase Profits by Using the Correct Products 16

    Products for Healthy Vending 17

    Maintain a high level of maintenance and customer service. 18

Chapter 2 21

Vending Machine Business Plan Template 21

    What Is a Business Plan? 21

    What is the Purpose of a Business Plan? 21

Source of Funding for Vending Machines 22

Template for a Vending Machine Business Plan 23

Chapter 3 38

Steps to Make Money from Vending Machines .. 38

What are the most profitable vending machine things to sell? 45

What is the best location for a vending machine? 46

Is a vending machine license required? 47

Chapter 4 49

The 10 Best Locations for Vending Machines 49

Can Vending Machines Be Installed in Any Location? 50

How to Select a Profitable Location for a Vending Machine 50

The Top Ten Vending Machine Locations 52

Chapter 5 60

What Type of Vending Machine Business is Right for You? 60

    Is the vending machine in good working order?.. 67

    Is there a selection of healthy snacks and beverages?... 68

Chapter 6 71

How to Be Successful in the Vending Business . 71

    Operating a Vending Machine Business Requirements 73

    Profits from Vending Machines................... 76

    Vending Machines' Top 4 Profitable Machines. 77

Chapter 7 82

Sales techniques that work in the vending machine business 82

    Before you initiate the first contact with a vending location owner/manager 83

    Analyze and manage your behavior............. 85

Blunders made by a new vending machine operator 90

Chapter 8 96

Tips on How to Grow Your Vending Machine Business 96

Trends in Vending Machines to Be Aware Of .. 99

Chapter 9 110

Types of Vending Machines for Your Business 110

The Internet of Things (IoT) Has Changed Vending Machines in 8 Ways 116

Chapter 10 127

Vending Machine Business Pros & Cons 127

How to Get a Vending Machine Permit 136

What is your role as a vending machine owner? 137

Profits are served up by next-generation vending machines. 137

Where does interest come from? 140

4 Things to Know About Vending Machine Card Readers 141

Introduction

Vending machines are used by customers for a variety of reasons. The majority of vending machines operate to satisfy public snack and beverage desires. By providing energy-boosting drinks, vending machines provide consumers with a quick and handy remedy for hunger pains or sluggish activities. As machine technology develops, the range of applications and demand for vending machines expands. Vending operations provide an entrepreneurial opportunity for anyone willing to put in the time and effort required to be successful.

Function

Vending machines are coin-operated machines that distribute items to customers. Vending machines are used by customers who pay for the goods within the machine and then use the items that are distributed. Machine operators generate money by installing machines in private businesses or public places in order to entice customers to buy something. Operators have specified routes for their machines, and it is their responsibility to service them and guarantee that they are stocked with the appropriate commodities.

Business Possibilities

1. Vending machine operators have a plethora of business opportunities. Entrepreneurs can buy an existing vending business, which usually comes with all of the necessary licenses, equipment, and routes already in place. Entrepreneurs can also buy a franchise or build a new company from the ground up. When buying an existing firm, the operator is responsible for keeping current accounts by providing services and filling the equipment with inventory. Entrepreneurs who want to start a new firm must buy or lease machines, buy inventory, and get permits and accounts to put the machines in place.

Types

1. Snack and soda vending machines are common. Individual candies or varied nuts are dispensed using smaller devices. In venues that cater to families and children, several machines are popular. Prizes and commodities that appeal to a younger audience are available on these machines. Vending machines that deliver rentable films are becoming increasingly common. Vending machines tailored to a certain market are also available. Self-serve vehicle washes, for example, have machines that provide disposable towels and individual auto detailing products.

Convenient Payment Options

1. Vending machine technology has advanced in recent years, allowing operators to provide more convenience to customers. Vending machines used to only accept coins or small denominations of currency, such as $1 or $5 bills. The types of payments accepted by vending machines have evolved as technology has progressed. Customers will find that certain vending machines now accept credit and debit cards as an extra convenience.

Advancements

1. Vending machines now sell a greater range of products. For example, at the Mondrian Hotel in Miami, a lavish vending machine lets customers to purchase products as extravagant as pricey jewelry, vehicles, and real estate. Vending services that have never been accessible before are in high demand.

Entrepreneurs have a unique opportunity to identify and capitalize on a vending niche that has yet to be established in the marketplace.

Chapter 1
How to Start a Vending Machine Business

Have you ever considered the economics of your office snacks? A vending machine business may be the appropriate choice for you if you're looking for a part-time business opportunity that requires no special skills or experience and that you can even incorporate your entire family into.

The vending machine industry in the United States was worth $8 billion just before the widespread COVID-19 shutdowns, and global vending machine income was worth $23 billion. Though the vending machine sector took a hit during the COVID-19 pandemic, it is projected to fully recover and even continue its growth pattern once people return to work and travel picks up again.

There are a lot of different things vending machines can do. You think they only give out chocolate bars and soda pop. This is a great time to start a vending machine business because there are new food and drink trends and more technology. Healthy snack options and niche offers are becoming more common in vending machines, and some cities have passed legislation requiring healthier vending machine options.

Gourmet foods like caviar, escargot, and bottarga can be bought from vending machines at Beverly Hills malls.

In order to start a vending machine business, you'll need to treat it like any other business that you start. You'll find everything you need to get going right here.

The Benefits of Owning a Vending Machine Business

The following are just a few of the many benefits of owning a vending machine business:

- **Scalability**: You can start with a few machines and scale up as time and resources allow.

- **Cheap initial expenses**: Your capital costs are quite low, aside from the machines, which can be financed. There's no need for a structure or office space; a garage, utility room, or basement can suffice. There is no need for any other equipment or machinery besides a truck to serve your route.

• **Ease of use**: Once the machines are set up, your sole responsibilities are to repair and replenish them as needed—and to collect the money.

• **All transactions involving cash**: In contrast to typical firms, there are no accounts receivable. Either you're collecting cash from the machines or you're collecting money from credit card firms.

• **Flexibility**: Families might consider starting a vending machine business. Purchases, stocking, bank deposits, bookkeeping, and other responsibilities can all be simply taught to your spouse and children.

Aside from a small amount of initial cash or funding, the only other prerequisite is a good level of physical condition, as servicing the machines entails a lot of walking and lugging products, some of which can be heavy.

If you believe that this is the correct business for you, here are the steps to take to establish your own vending machine company.

Starting a vending machine business has a number of drawbacks.

However, there are certain drawbacks to owning and operating a vending machine business. Here are some things to think about before you start one:

• Competition

• Requires moderate maintenance (restocking machines and machine repair on occasion)

• Expensive delivery fees (for receiving the machine and taking it to the location)

Complete your homework

Market research and planning, like with any form of business, are essential for success. There are several ways to establish a vending machine business, each with its own set of benefits and drawbacks.

How to start from the Ground Up

You have the most freedom when you buy equipment and source locations yourself—you may start with a few units and expand as opportunities and money allow. It also necessitates the most legwork, since you'll need to discover and negotiate places for machines as well as source and acquire them (unless you deal with a machine distributor who sells machines and provides locations).

Purchasing an existing vending machine business or vending machine route

This solution allows you to receive quick income flow from your current business. However, it's critical to figure out why the owner wants to sell. Examining the accounts, inspecting the machines, examining current contracts, and investigating the existing sites for potential difficulties are all important aspects of background research.

Purchasing a Business Franchise

This is the most straightforward approach to enter the vending machine industry. A franchise provides you with a proven business strategy centered on the sale of a certain product or products. In most cases, however, the franchisor gets a share of the profits or a monthly charge in addition to the beginning franchise fee. You are often limited to acquiring or renting machines and products from the franchising business as a franchisee.

You must obtain the essential licenses and permissions, as well as register your firm for tax purposes, as with any profit-making venture. Make sure you're up to date on all federal, state, and local regulations.

The following stage, regardless of the choice you choose, should be to draft a business strategy. Market research is an important aspect of your business strategy since it helps you determine whether your business idea is viable. You might discover, for example, that the market for vending machines in your area is already saturated by reviewing existing vending machine locations and interacting with business owners.

Find out where the machines are and sign contracts.

In the vending machine business, as in retail and real estate, location is very important. You should put your machines in places where a lot of people go, like malls, big office buildings, schools, airports, and in front of stores.5

You want good sites that don't already have vending machines in the best case scenario. However, you'll undoubtedly find that most of the best spots in your region are already taken, and that existing vendors may have exclusive contracts with the property owner in some circumstances.

Keep in mind that even if you have the ideal location, your product selection must be appropriate. Even well-known products may fail to sell in a high-traffic area if the target market is insufficient.

A candy vending machine in front of a health food store might not be the best idea.

Vandalism and Theft

When scouting venues, make sure to look up crime statistics and stay away from regions where theft and vandalism are common. Your revenues will be soon depleted due to damage or theft. Locations that are preferred should be highly visible, patrolled, and monitored by security cameras.

Contracts

You'll have to pay compensation to business or property owners for putting devices on their property and using their power. This is usually done as a percentage of your gross sales that is negotiated.

The average charge is roughly 7%, however it varies significantly based on the quantity and size of machines. You will be required by contract to give a statement of sales and commissions to the business or property owner at regular intervals as the machine owner.

Your contract should also include the following information:

- Machine types and products offered
- Contract term
- Termination clauses for contract breach or unprofitability
- Exclusivity (if applicable)
- Rights to replace, raise, or decrease the number of machines

It's usually a good idea to have a lawyer draft or review the contract.

Equipment Purchase or Leasing

If you're not buying an existing firm or franchising, you'll need to buy one or more machines to get started. You must first pick what products you want to sell (food, beverage, or speciality items), as well as what type of vending machines you want.

Machines for Bulk Production

These are little vending machines that dispense handfuls of bulk food items like gumballs, peanuts, and M&Ms. Costs may range from $50 to $200, with the smallest profit margins possible. To make a significant profit, you'd need a lot more machines. On the plus side, the machines don't need to be refilled as frequently and are easy to maintain and repair.

Machines that work mechanically

These machines are bigger than bulk machines and may dispense a variety of items. Although prices start at $2,000 per machine, profit margins are significantly better than with bulk machines. There are eight electronic machines.

These make use of current touch screens and can accept a variety of payment methods, including bills and credit cards. Electronic devices are the most expensive upfront, but they are also the most reliable. A new basic computerized Coke dispensing equipment will set you back at least $3,000. More advanced machines with a higher capacity, various products, and several payment methods can quickly double or triple the cost.

Unfortunately, because vending machines are frequently left unattended, they are vulnerable to damage and theft. If you spend a lot of money on an equipment, you should consider insuring it.

Purchasing Second-Hand Equipment

Used machines are the way to go if you're wanting to start small or simply save money on a discounted product. There are a variety of places to look for information:

• Craigslist is an excellent place to look for locally available machines, and UsedVending.com is a great place to look for used vending machines. You can run thorough equipment searches depending on kind, price, and location.

• Amazon and eBay are also good places to look for new and secondhand vending machines. The reviews are very useful for product reliability information.

• Vending machine sellers are available, so look for them on the internet or in local business journals.

Repairs and Warranty

A one- or two-year components warranty is usually included with new vending machines. Used or remanufactured equipment may have a shorter warranty period.

You can learn to repair the equipment yourself if you are mechanically inclined. You may need to hire a repair professional if this is not the case.

Increase Profits by Using the Correct Products

Inquire about the products desired by the business or property owners. The sort of products will be part of the contract in some situations.

You should also consider the location and intended market. Some products do well in most public places, whereas others are more location-dependent:

• In most contexts, hot drinks such as coffee, tea, and hot chocolate may sell well, as may snack machine vending products such as sodas, water, candies, chips, and chocolate bars.

• It might be better for businesses or schools to have hot meal and sandwich machines that make food like soup and sandwiches. Candy and other specialist machines might be better for stores and other places where people go to buy food.

• Personal things such as hygiene products and over-the-counter drugs may be permitted in public toilets, malls, and service stations.

Products for Healthy Vending

Healthy options may be required by law in your jurisdiction. There are a variety of choices, including:

• Salads and fresh sandwiches

• Instead of sodas, drink water or fruit juices.

• Baked chips instead of candy

• Granola bars

• Fruit cups

- Sugar-free gum
- Nuts

Obtaining Products

Pay the lowest possible per-unit pricing for the commodities you buy for your vending machines to maximize your vending machine profitability. Costco, for example, is a good place to start looking for wholesale food and drink providers and comparing pricing. If at all possible, negotiate bulk discounts.

Maintain a high level of maintenance and customer service.

Success in the vending machine industry, like any other business, depends on offering excellent customer service. For a vending machine operator, this means:

- Make periodic visits to your locations to ensure that the machines are well stocked.

- Make sure your machines are clean and in good working order. Customers are turned off by dirty, poorly maintained devices.

- Provide contact information on the machines, such as an email address, so that customers can report any problems.

- Rotate products by sell-by dates, if relevant, so that the oldest inventory sells first.

- Analyze sales and advise with business or property owners on which types of products are most appealing to customers on a regular basis. Ensure that the machines are properly stocked.

- Maintain strong ties with the machine location's contact person, as they may be the recipient of complaints or refund requests.

- Maintain a professional demeanor at all times.

Providing excellent customer service is one of the most effective methods to boost sales and improve your company's reputation, both of which are necessary if you want to expand your company by seeking out new locations for equipment.

Final Thoughts

There are few hurdles to getting into the vending machine business. What you'll need the most is what any starting company needs: dedication and a drive to succeed.

People who run vending machine businesses aren't likely to be rich, just like people who run small businesses aren't likely to be rich, either On the other hand, being your own boss and making the decisions is a good thing in and of itself.

Vending machines can also provide a regular revenue if you set up enough sites.

Chapter 2
Vending Machine Business Plan Template

What Is a Business Plan?

A business plan gives you a glimpse of your vending machine right now and lays out your five-year growth strategy. It defines your company's objectives and how you plan to achieve them. Market research is also included to back up your plans.

What is the Purpose of a Business Plan?

A business plan is required if you want to start a vending machine business or expand an existing vending machine business. A business plan will assist you in raising funds if necessary and planning the expansion of your vending machine business to increase your chances of success. Your vending machine business plan should be updated on a yearly basis as your firm develops and evolves.

Source of Funding for Vending Machines

Personal savings, credit cards, bank loans, and angel investors are the most common sources of capital for a vending machine business. When it comes to bank loans, banks will want to look over your company plan to make sure you'll be able to repay the loan and interest. The loan officer will not simply want to ensure that your financials are reasonable in order to gain this confidence. They will, however, expect to see a competent plan. They will be more confident in your ability to run a business successfully and professionally if you have a plan like this.

Angel investors are the second most popular source of finance for a vending machine company. Wealthy individuals who will write you a cheque are known as angel investors. They will either want equity in exchange for their capital or will provide you with a loan, similar to a bank. A vending machine business will not be funded by venture investors.

Template for a Vending Machine Business Plan

The following ten sections should be included in your business plan:

Summary of the Report

Your executive summary serves as an introduction to your business plan, although it is usually written last because it summarizes each of the plan's major sections.

The purpose of your Executive Summary is to draw the reader in fast. Explain to them what type of vending machine business you have and where you are in the process of growing it; for example, are you a startup, do you have a vending machine business that you want to expand, or do you run a vending machine chain?

After that, give an outline of each of your plan's future components. Give a quick overview of the vending machine industry, for example. Talk about the type of vending machine business you have. Describe your direct competitors in detail. Give a brief description of your target market. Give an overview of your marketing strategy. Determine who the most important individuals of your team are. Also, provide a summary of your financial strategy.

Analyze the Business

You will describe the type of vending machine you operate in your company analysis.

For instance, you might run one of the following businesses:

1. **Food and snacks**: pre-packaged foods like chips and cookies, as well as perishable items like sandwiches, ice cream, and fruit, are common in this type of vending machine business.

2. **Beverages**: this sort of vending machine can serve hot or cold beverages (coffee, chocolate) (soft drinks, water)

3. **Candies**: candy and gum are the only items available in this sort of vending machine.

4. **Other products**: these might include healthy food options (granola, fruit, hummus, and so on),

as well as consumer goods like electronics, movies, condoms, and souvenirs.

The Company Analysis portion of your business plan should include information on the business in addition to outlining the type of vending machine you operate.

Include responses to questions like:

• When and why did you establish your company?

• What achievements have you made thus far? Milestones could include sales targets met, new machine locations, and so on.

• Your legal framework. Are you an S-Corp or a C-Corp? What is a limited liability company (LLC)? What exactly is a sole proprietorship? Here's where you'll explain your legal structure.

Analysis of the Industry

You must include an overview of the vending machine industry in your industry analysis.

While this may appear to be redundant, it serves a number of reasons.

To begin, learn about the vending machine industry by conducting research. It assists you in comprehending the market in which you operate.

Second, market research can help you improve your approach, especially if it recognizes market trends. If there is a trend toward selling advertising on vending machines, for example, you should make sure your plan allows for a variety of ad styles and sizes.

The third purpose for conducting market research is to demonstrate to readers that you are an industry expert. You accomplish this by performing research and presenting it in your strategy.

In the industry study portion of your vending machine business plan, you should answer the following questions:

• What is the size of the vending machine industry (in terms of dollars)?

• Is the market on the decline or on the rise?

• Who are the market's main competitors?

- Who are the market's major suppliers?
- What are the current industry trends?
- How do you expect the industry to grow in the next 5-10 years?
- What is the size of the relevant market? That is, how large is your vending machine's potential market? You may estimate a figure like this by calculating the size of the national market and then applying that value to your local population.

Analysis of the Client

The clients you serve and/or expect to serve must be detailed in the customer analysis portion of your vending machine business plan.

Hotels, business complexes, correctional facilities, and other customer sectors are examples.

As you might expect, the sort of vending machine you operate will be heavily influenced by the consumer segment(s) you select. Clearly, correctional facilities will desire different price and product options than office buildings, and will respond to various marketing initiatives.

Try to segment your target market based on their demographic and psychographic characteristics. Include a description of the ages, genders, localities, and income levels of the clients you intend to serve (both end customers (who purchase things from your vending machines) and decision-makers) when it comes to demographics (who approve your desire to place a vending machine in their facility).

Psychographic profiles describe your target clients' wants and demands. The better you understand and identify these needs, the more likely you are to attract and retain customers.

Analysis of Competitors

Your competitive study should identify your company's indirect and direct competitors, with the latter receiving the most attention.

Other vending machines are **direct competitors**.

Customers have alternative possibilities to purchase from you **besides direct competitors**, which are known as indirect competitors. This includes fast food restaurants, convenience stores, grocery stores, pharmacies, and pharmacies. You must mention this competition to demonstrate that you are aware that not everyone who buys convenience items utilizes a vending machine on a daily basis.

You should describe the other vending machine firms with which you compete in terms of direct competition. Vending machines positioned near your location will most likely be your direct competitors.

Provide an overview of each competitor's business and a list of their strengths and flaws. It will be hard to know everything there is to know about your competition unless you have already worked for them. However, you should be able to learn important details about them, such as:

• Who do they serve as customers?

- What services do they provide?

- How do they charge (premium, inexpensive, etc.)?

- What do they excel at?

- What are their drawbacks?

Consider your responses to the last two questions from the standpoint of your customers.

Documenting your areas of competitive advantage is the final portion of your competitive analysis section. Consider the following scenario:

- Will you be able to deliver outstanding products?

- Are you going to offer things that your competitors don't?

- Will you make purchasing your products easier or faster for customers?

- Are you going to improve your customer service?

- Will you be able to provide better pricing?

Consider how you can exceed your competitors and write them down in this portion of your plan.

Marketing Strategy

A marketing strategy typically incorporates the four Ps: product, price, location, and promotion. Your marketing plan for a vending machine business plan should include the following:

Product: Reiterate the type of vending machine business you described in your Company Analysis in the product area. Then, go into depth about the precise things you'll be selling. Will you, for example, offer vending machines that sell coffee or other consumer goods in addition to snack machines?

Price: Make a list of the prices you'll be offering and how they compare to those of your competitors. The product and price sub-sections of your marketing plan are essentially where you present the things you sell and their prices.

The position of your vending machine is referred to as "**place**." Make a note of where you're going and how it'll affect your success. Is your vending machine, for example, placed in a high-trafficked office building or gym? Discuss how you can ensure a consistent flow of clients at your site.

Promotions: The promotions area is the last phase of your vending machine marketing strategy. You'll write about how you'll get customers to your store in this section (s). You might want to think about the following strategies of promotion:

• Keeping your vending machine clean and appealing to passers-by in order to attract passing customers

• focusing on machine design and technology for a better user experience

• strategically placing vending machines

Plan of Action

While the goals in the previous sections of your company plan were described, your operations plan explains how you will achieve them. Your operations strategy should be divided into two portions, as shown below.

All of the operations involved in running your vending machine, such as sourcing products, transporting and replenishing, maintaining the machines clean, and so on, are included in daily **short-term processes**.

Long-term objectives are the milestones you want to reach. These could be the dates when you plan to install your tenth machine or when you aim to meet a sales goal of $X. It might also be the date on which you plan to hire your Xth employee or open a new location.

Management Group

A competent management team is required to demonstrate your vending machine's capacity to succeed as a business. Highlight the backgrounds of your key individuals, stressing the talents and experiences that demonstrate their aptitude to create a business.

You and/or your team members should ideally have direct vending machine experience. If this is the case, emphasize your knowledge and experience. However, you should also mention any experience that you believe will aid in the success of your company.

Consider forming an advisory board if your team is inadequate. An advisory board would consist of 2 to 8 people who would act as mentors to your company. They'd be able to answer queries and offer strategic advice. Look for members of the advisory board who have experience with vending machines and/or successfully running retail and small enterprises, if necessary.

Plan your money.

The first year of your financial plan should have your five-year financial statement broken down into monthly or quarterly summaries. Then it should be broken down into annual summaries for the rest of the years. It is part of your financial statements to show how much money you made or spent and how much money you made or spent.

Profit and Loss Statement (P&L): An income statement is sometimes known as a profit and loss statement. It displays your revenues before subtracting your expenses to determine whether you made a profit.

You'll need to make assumptions when creating your income statement. Will you serve 50 or 100 consumers per day, for example? Will sales increase by 2% or 10% per year? As you can expect, the assumptions you choose will have a significant impact on the financial estimates for your company. Conduct as much research as possible to try to ground your assumptions in truth.

Balance Sheets: While balance sheets contain a lot of information, they reveal your assets and liabilities, which is the most important thing to know. For example, spending $100,000 to expand your vending machine business will not result in instant earnings. It's more of an asset that will ideally help you make money for years to come. Similarly, if a bank issues you a check for $100,000, you are not required to pay it back right once. Rather, it is a debt that you will repay over time.

Statement of Cash Flows: Your cash flow statement can help you figure out how much money you'll need to start or grow your firm, as well as ensure that you never run out. Most entrepreneurs and business owners are unaware that it is possible to make a profit while simultaneously running out of cash and going bankrupt.

Include several key costs in your Income Statement and Balance Sheets when starting or growing a vending machine:

• Cost of equipment such as vending machines, refrigerated delivery trucks, etc.

• Cost of maintaining an adequate amount of inventory

• Payroll or salaries paid to employees

• Business insurance

• Taxes and permits

Appendix

In the appendix of your plan, include your complete financial predictions as well as any supporting documentation that can help your plan stand out. You may, for example, include the design plan for your delivery truck or the specifications of your equipment leasing.

Summary of the Vending Machine Business Plan

It's a good idea to put together a business strategy for your vending machine company. If you follow the template above, you will be a true expert by the time you are finished. You'll have a thorough understanding of the vending machine industry, as well as your competitors and customers. You'll have created a marketing strategy and will have a thorough understanding of what it takes to start and grow a vending machine business.

Chapter 3

Steps to Make Money from Vending Machines

To start your own vending machine business, you'll need to follow ten basic steps.

Step 1: Create a business plan.

To begin, draft a business strategy that outlines your aims and objectives.

While writing a business plan may appear to be a time-consuming task, it is critical and should not be overlooked. Here are some easy steps to follow while writing a vending machine business plan:

• Define your company: What type of vending machine business will you run?

• Define your objectives and make sure they're quantifiable and achievable.

• Conduct a market analysis: for example, look into your local competitors.

- Go over all areas of the business, such as marketing and strategy.

Keep in mind that you'll be tracking your progress, profits, and losses while you create your company plan. These should be documented in a profit and loss statement, which is a financial document that emphasizes your business's income and costs and allows you to calculate a profit or loss at the end of each month and year.

A profit and loss statement will assist you in immediately identifying income opportunities and expenses, as well as providing an overview of how your organization is performing financially over time.

Step 2: Decide on a location.

Next, decide where you'll put your vending machine or vending machines.

Consider potential locations, surrounding anchor stores, traffic on that street, and any other criteria that can assist you assess whether or not you've chosen a good location.

Vending machines work best in settings where people have to wait, where there is a lot of foot traffic, and where there is residential and/or commercial property, such as apartment complexes or doctor's offices.

You can either use a relocation service or discover a good site on your own, which we'll discuss more in step three.

Step 3: Make contact with businesses and negotiate with them.

If you want to locate a vending machine on your own, you'll need to make contact with local businesses to set up a partnership.

This requires approaching business owners and requesting permission to install your vending machine at their location, such as an auto repair shop. Make an agreement with them that includes providing them a percentage of your sales proceeds, such as 5% every month, in exchange for the space your machine will occupy.

Request to talk with the owner or management via phone or in person. Explain how the agreement would be a win-win situation for everyone when you make your request. You will profit financially from having your vending machine installed in a business, and the proprietor will profit from a share of your sales.

Step 4: Hire a contractor to fix the problem.

Then you should think about what you'll do if your vending machines break down. This is where finding a competent repairman comes into play.

At this point, you should conduct some study. Find a maintenance person with a good reputation and who would be available if your vending machine broke down. Vending machines, unfortunately, can stop working at any time.

Place an out-of-order sign on your computer until it can be repaired if it can't be serviced right away.

Step 5: Invest in (or rent) vending machines

This can be a costly investment that will pay off in the long run.

Vending machines can be purchased online or in person. You'll definitely discover vending machines faster online, but shipping charges may make them pricier. Because these machines are large and heavy, delivering them domestically to your location will almost certainly cost you a lot of money, though some merchants do provide free delivery.

You can buy machines through marketplace websites or online merchants if you go the online route. You can also buy from a variety of industry websites, such as Vending.com and others.

You might also think about buying old vending machines. If you compare the cost of factory-remanufactured vending machines to the cost of new vending machines, you can save a lot of money. Some sellers of old machines also provide limited warranties, financing, and other services.

Take your time looking over your selections because this is a significant expenditure and one of the most crucial company investments you'll make.

Step 6: Place Your Vending Machines

Once you've decided where you want your machine to go, it's time to get it there. You can haul it yourself in an SUV or truck, or you can rent a delivery vehicle from Budget, U-Haul, or another provider. Finally, you might engage a delivery firm to carry the machine for you, which is an excellent choice if you are unable to do so yourself.

Step 7: Examine Your Earnings

Remember that you should be producing enough money from the equipment to cover all of your expenses, including:

- Rent
- Repairs
- Inventory
- Transportation

Continue to assess your costs and profits on a regular basis to verify that the vending machine location you selected is lucrative.

If not, it's time to renegotiate your rent, relocate to a better location for your firm, or find other measures to boost your profit margins.

Step 8: Make sure your vending machines are fully stocked and operational.

Keeping your vending machines well-stocked and in good functioning order is a crucial element of the vending machine company. The food, toys, or other products you're selling, as well as the dollar bill and change container, are all included.

It's all about upkeep in this line of work. Check on your machines frequently, or employ someone to visit your locations to ensure that they are operational and stocked.

Step 9: Invest in Your Company

Consider your long-term goals, including measures to boost your bottom line, when you write your company strategy.

Consider reinvesting your income to expand your vending machine business and buy new machines, allowing you to expand into other markets.

Step 10: Building an Emergency Fund.

Building an emergency fund for your firm, which will cover unforeseen costs such as repairs, is the final stage to consider. It's critical to keep cash on hand in case of a business emergency that necessitates capital injection.

What are the most profitable vending machine things to sell?

Some instances are as follows:

• Name-brand sodas, such as Coke and Pepsi; name-brand snacks and candies, such as Snickers, Lays Chips, and Sun bar, and so on.

• Cold foods, such as sandwiches

• Ice

• Toys

• Gumballs

At Costco, a 35-pack of Sprite costs around $14. You may then resell each can for $1.50, netting $52.50 on the full pack - a $38.50 profit!

It costs $24 for a 30-pack of full-size candy bars. Selling them at $2 each will net you $60, a $36 profit.

More importantly, you can boost your profit margin by purchasing your products from a wholesaler rather than a retailer.

What is the best location for a vending machine?

Here are some possible locations for a vending machine:

- Service locations
- Commercial office spaces
- Waiting areas
- Hotels
- Shopping malls
- Strip malls
- Auto dealerships

Is a vending machine license required?

A vending machine business may require a business permission or license, depending on your location.

Is it possible to start a vending machine business for nothing?

If you currently own a business where you may place one or more vending machines, you can establish a vending machine business for free.

If you want a bigger slice of the pie or want to start your own vending machine business, you'll need to spend in the machine itself, as well as the things you sell and the maintenance.

Is it wise to invest in vending machines?

When compared to the average beginning cost for traditional enterprises, which can vary greatly, a vending machine business can be started for less than $500.

Even if you start with many or more expensive machines, you will most likely make a profit within the first three years. This is a pretty simple business to operate, with a low entrance barrier.

The procedure of scaling up is likewise rather simple. Simply repeat the steps you went through to get new devices and position them in more locations for an immediate increase in revenue.

Chapter 4
The 10 Best Locations for Vending Machines

Entrepreneurs are drawn to vending businesses because they offer flexible hours and the option to scale up or down according to their needs. Additionally, it enables entrepreneurs to operate in a semi-absentee capacity, which many entrepreneurs find appealing.

According to vendingmarketwatch.com, the United States currently has about 1.8 million vending machines, which generate over $13.3 billion in annual revenue.

However, collecting revenue from vending machines while you sleep requires effort. The first step toward developing a profitable vending business is selecting the appropriate site. A vending machine that is not visible to the public will not produce income. If you're considering beginning a vending machine business, this article will teach you how to choose successful locations.

Can Vending Machines Be Installed in Any Location?

While a vending machine might theoretically be placed everywhere, the reality is more complicated. To begin, you cannot lawfully place a machine on another person's property or use their utilities without first obtaining their permission or entering into a contract. Second, not all vending machine locations are optimal. What good is an idle vending machine with no customers? It is critical to locate the most profitable potential locations when starting or developing a vending business.

How to Select a Profitable Location for a Vending Machine

As with the real estate market, success in the vending industry is all about location, location, location. A lucrative business begins with the selection of the appropriate locations, which requires some research and homework to assess traffic, analyze your competition, and obtain permission from property owners.

Traffic

Without customers, a vending business cannot be viable. A vending machine's success is highly dependent on foot traffic. Keep in mind that vending machine purchases frequently fall into two categories: impulse purchases and routine purchases. People either grab something when they are in need of a fast pick-me-up and a snack catches their attention, or they develop the habit of purchasing from a machine they see on a daily basis, such as in their break room at work, school, or apartment or condo building.

Permissions

It would be fantastic if you could simply plug in a vending machine and start generating money immediately. To place your machines, however, you will want permission from property owners and a contract.

In some circumstances, securing a contract will be straightforward, but in others, you will need to jump through several hoops. In many cases, business owners will additionally request a portion of the revenues generated by your devices in order to offset the cost of their utilities and produce some passive income of their own.

The Top Ten Vending Machine Locations

What are some of the greatest vending machine locations? Each location considered by a vending operator should be analyzed separately, however the following are 10 of the most desirable places.

Establishments of manufacture or distribution

Vending machines are an excellent addition to manufacturing facilities, industrial parks, and distribution hubs. Typically, these establishments employ hundreds of workers throughout many shifts (typically 24 hours a day). Numerous facilities provide brief breaks, and employees rarely has time to visit a restaurant off-site. Adding vending machines to the break room offers them with options – and provides a regular source of revenue for the vending business.

Offices

Vending machines are an excellent fit for businesses with 50 or more employees. Employees experience hunger and thirst throughout the day, and vending machines provide options for those who do not bring their own beverages, snacks, or lunches, which is the majority of individuals in today's hectic environment.

Apartment Complexes

Apartment complexes are a whirlwind of activity, with residents arriving and departing 24 hours a day, 7 days a week. Numerous complexes also provide laundry facilities, common areas, playgrounds and parks, as well as party rooms and gymnasiums. These are excellent places for vending machines since they are accessible to all members of the community and are frequently used by numerous residents. Vending machines featuring a diverse assortment of food and beverage products can be placed in one or more locations across the property.

Hospitals

Hospitals are always open for business. They are open twenty-four hours a day, seven days a week, and 365 days a year. Additionally, they appeal to three unique customer categories. Vendors can provide a welcome diversion from conventional cuisine for patients. Caretakers and employees like the convenience and variety offered by vending machines–they also lack the time to venture outside the facility to eat. Finally, guests who are visiting and caring for loved ones frequently rely on vending machines for a quick snack, allowing them to spend more time with them. Being open 24 hours a day, seven days a week, with numerous shifts and multiple buyers is a perfect mix for vending machine earnings.

Care Facilities / Nursing Homes

Nursing homes and assisted living facilities, like hospitals, are open 24 hours a day, 365 days a year. Residents appreciate the variety of refreshments available, while visitors rely on vending machines for a fast lunch or snack to allow them to spend more time with their loved ones. Finally, the majority of nursing home caregivers work extended shifts with few breaks. This makes vending an ideal option for recharging their batteries throughout their shift. All of these elements contribute to the place being extremely profitable and popular.

Automobile Manufacturers

When visiting a car lot/dealership to look at autos, the average consumer will spend approximately three hours. Additionally, these locations receive a significant volume of foot traffic and operate on a 24-hour basis. Apart from car sales, the majority of dealerships also have well equipped service departments with average wait times of 1.5 to 3 hours. Not to mention that sales representatives, technicians, and service personnel all rely on vending machines for quick food and beverage alternatives. All of these variables contribute to the fact that car dealerships are one of the highest-grossing vending machine locations. Additionally, the majority of auto dealerships are part of a bigger family of dealerships, which provides you with the ideal opportunity to extend your business into other markets.

Resorts and Inns

The guests of hotels and motels are captive markets. Even though a hotel has a restaurant, not every guest desires or desires a complete meal. While some hotels feature micro markets, they are often located in the lobby, and not every visitor wants to make the trip for a quick snack — especially if one is located on their floor. Installing vending machines in the foyer, side entrances, and ice machine areas might be an excellent method to create steady money.

Gyms

Gym-goers work up an appetite, and they don't necessarily want to stop at the drive-thru next door for something unhealthy; they want something nutritious. Gyms and fitness facilities are perfect sites for vending machines that sell healthy snacks and beverages to help consumers replenish following a workout. Another reason employees love having a vending machine with healthy options is that most of them work for a few hours a week and have very little time off.

Schools, community colleges, and universities all have different ways for people to learn.

Students are a feisty bunch – and they eat well. Every single day, schools, community colleges, and universities are humming with activity. Having vending machines in strategic places on a school's property can make a lot of money because a lot of people pass by each day who are in a hurry, hungry, and want a quick snack while they work between classes or hurry to get to class. Parents and school administrators want to make sure that their kids have healthy snacks available to them during the school day, so vending machines that sell healthy foods are a good idea for schools.

Vending machines also work well in college dorms. Students stay up late and are not always in the mood to run out for a snack while working or socializing with their friends. When a vending machine can accept bank cards, credit cards, or even school meal plan cards, it's even easier to go to the machine and buy something quick.

Supermarkets

Vending machines are used by two different groups of people in a store. To start, let's think about the people who come and go from the store. People often get hungry and thirsty while running errands, and putting a vending machine near an entrance can be a great way to get people to come in and buy things on impulse.

The second audience segment is comprised of current and prospective employees. Retail employees typically receive one or two ten-minute breaks and a brief meal break during their shifts. They frequently lack the time to run to a restaurant for a meal or snack, and vending machines provide a convenient way for them to refuel before returning to the floor.

Chapter 5

What Type of Vending Machine Business is Right for You?

The first thing you should think about before starting a vending machine business is where you will put your machines. After you've done your market research and chosen your sites, the next question is what kind of vending machines you'll need to offer the proper products to your clients. There are several varieties to select from, so have a look at some of them below and learn about the benefits and drawbacks of each to see which one best meets your needs.

Vending of Bulk Candy

M&Ms, gumballs, Skittles, Mike & Ike's, and possibly small stickers or toys in clear globe encasing are all available in these machines. The customer usually receives 7 to 10 pieces of candy for 25 cents.

The Advantages of Bulk Vending Machines

These machines may be a good alternative for you if you are new to the vending machine company. You may acquire a machine for $150 to $450, so even if you don't have a lot of money to invest at first, you can get into the vending machine business by picking bulk candy vending machines. Profit margins on the products inside these machines are extremely high. A gumball from the wholesale store may cost you 2 to 5 cents, while a consumer will spend 25 cents for the identical gumball from your vending machine. If you have a large number of machines and strategically place them, you can quickly recoup your initial investment.

If you sell a product for less than a specific price, you may not have to pay any sales tax at all in many states. Because most bulk vending machines have few mechanical parts, repairing a broken one does not need expertise. Businesses are more likely to allow you to install this type of vending machine because it uses no power and takes up little space.

The Drawbacks of Bulk Vending Machines

If you rely on bulk vending machines to produce a considerable profit, it may take longer unless you have a large number of sites. To justify the expenditures of your time and gasoline going to the sites to reload the machines, you'll probably have to cluster them within a limited radius. Because bulk vending machines are light, they are sometimes stolen, so make sure yours is in a highly visible location with plenty of foot traffic.

Even if your bulk vending machines are miles apart, you may still save money on gas and time spent in the van by using vending management software to predict when a machine will need service and how to determine the best path to them.

Vending Machines for Snacks and Soda

These vending machines are generally the first that come to mind when people think of vending machines because they can be found almost anywhere - at malls, companies, on the highway, in parks, and at highway rest stops, to mention a few places.

Vending Machines for Snacks and Soda Have Their Advantages

The commodities in these machines have a higher dollar value than candy vending machines. You can make a $1 or more on each item purchased instead of 20 cents. This results in a higher profit margin, and you don't need as many machines to make a decent profit. These machines are heavier, which is a good thing because it makes them harder to steal, but it can be an issue when moving them from one site to another.

However, if you can locate a feasible, well-established vending location for such a machine, you could make a lot of money. Because you earn more per machine than if you operated candy vending machines, your route can cover a greater area, possibly up to 50 miles.

Again, by carefully assessing the product mix that you require at each site, vending management software may help you maximize sales turnover. Knowing the exact product quantities that each machine requires will assist you in loading delivery trucks more efficiently, saving you time and effort.

Vending Machines for Snacks and Soda Have Drawbacks

These machines are more expensive than bulk vending machines, and depending on the age of the device, you can expect to pay anywhere from $1,500 to $8,500 per machine. It will cost less than a brand new item if it has been refurbished or used, but it should still produce the same results. Because these devices use power, potential location owners may be hesitant to allow you to set up shop on their property. Paying the owner a tiny commission is one way to get around this.

Snack and soda machines, particularly those in less-than-ideal settings, are occasionally vandalized. It is preferable to place the unit at a prominent area within a building to avoid vandalism. Furthermore, when a machine is outside, harsh weather has the potential to damage the interior components. Because these huge machines have more parts than a bulk vending machine, you'll need to understand how to perform simple repairs and who to call for help if you have a major problem. The longer it's out of commission, the less money your vending machine company makes.

Vending Machines of Other Types

There are more types of vending machine businesses than bulk candy vending and snacks and soda vending, but we've focused on those two here because they're the most popular. There are far too many vending machine business possibilities to list them all, but some options include coffee and hot beverage machines, change machines, vending machines for toiletries and medical supplies, and vending machines for office supplies. Although snack and drink vending machines are frequently the first to come to mind, customers looking for specific products in various settings and environments have a variety of possibilities.

A business owner may choose to start with one or two vending machines and expand when they begin to make a profit, or they may want to use multiple versions of the same vending machine, or even different sorts of vending machines, in various settings and for various target audiences. If you're new to this type of business, you might want to think about one of the above possibilities, carefully weighing the benefits and drawbacks of each and completing additional study before making your final selection.

Once you've chosen the vending machine type that best suits your needs and positioned them in their proper locations, you must rapidly determine if these are the suitable machines for the job. What exactly is the "correct" machine? Remember, it's your money and your business on the line, therefore machine performance analysis must begin right away. A machine type that produces a specific product mix may operate effectively in one location but fail terribly in another. So, how do you assess and evaluate their work? How can you keep track of your complete inventory's sales without missing a beat? Is the machine's performance enough or might it be better? What are the best-selling things and what are the slow-moving items that need to be removed? Using vending machine software, you may get instant answers to all of these queries. **Three Things Your Customers Want to Know About Vending Machines**

Many people avoid vending machines since the contents are occasionally suspect, and there are no alternatives for fresh produce from a home-cooked meal. Nutritious vending machines, on the other hand, may give quick snacks, and many of the goods and components are both healthy and convenient. What are the things that people search for and what are their concerns?

Is the vending machine in good working order?

Dusty machines, empty coils, expired product, and burned-out bulbs are all signs of a vending operator who is having difficulty managing their business. Your healthy vending business's first impression must create trust in the customer, or they will carry on with their day without ever stopping by.

Tactical Tip: Take a few moments to clean, organize, sort, and maintain each of your vending machines as you visit them. To potential healthy vending customers, its first impression is crucial.

Is there a selection of healthy snacks and beverages?

It's not only a pleasant feature to have access to nutritional information for snacks and drinks; it's soon becoming a legal requirement. When a consumer is hungry or thirsty, updated technology like AirVend, which shows inventory nutritional information, helps offer them the knowledge they need to make a healthy selection.

Tactical Tip: To keep in compliance with regulatory obligations as well as client preferences, make sure your inventory is properly set up with nutritional information.

Is it possible for me to pay using the means I have?

Younger professionals rarely carry cash; instead, they rely on debit and credit cards to make transactions. Allowing consumers to utilize the payment methods that are most convenient for them will result in them spending more money and doing it more frequently.

Being a successful healthy vending operator also necessitates the use of cash. If you're using dollars and coins, make sure you have enough change. There's nothing more aggravating to a potential buyer than reading an alert that says "precise change only" and then being denied their purchase.

Tactical Tip: Use telemetry devices for credit and debit card processing. Check your bill validators and coin boxes to make sure your machine is always stocked with enough cash.

Final Thoughts

Your vending customers want to put their trust in you. They want to rely on you to fill in the gaps in their day and to assist them when they are hungry or thirsty. You'll be a more successful vending business owner if you know what they desire.

Chapter 6

How to Be Successful in the Vending Business

The location of a vending machine is the most critical determinant in its profitability. A vending machine with mediocre items in a high-traffic area will generate more money than one with delicious foods that no one sees. Your machines should ideally offer highly appealing items and be located in a high-traffic area for optimal earnings. If you don't keep your machines stocked and maintained, you'll lose sales.

1. Establish relationships with business owners and merchants in high-traffic areas. Give them a reason to let you put your machines in their stores by offering them a discount. This is frequently accomplished by giving them a portion of your revenue.

2. Find out where the best vending machine locations are in your region, and note which machines are currently there. A drink machine

should not be placed adjacent to another drink machine. Both you and the owner of the other machine will lose money as a result of this. Place machines next to each other that sell complementary things, such as a candy machine next to a drink machine.

3. Locate your machines in places that form an easy-to-navigate driving path, as you'll be traveling the route frequently to service and resupply your equipment. Don't put a single machine too far away from the others; this will limit cost effectiveness.

4. Obtain instruction in vending machine mechanics. You will save money by not having to hire a professional if you understand them and can correct faults yourself.

5. Experiment with different vending machine products. You will substantially lessen competition from other vending machines and generate more money if you can come up with things that sell well and give diversity. Expand your product line

beyond food to include small toys, personal care goods, stamps, and other miscellaneous items.

Operating a Vending Machine Business Requirements

The vending machine company can be profitable, but it's not something you should get into without doing some study first. Some of the prerequisites for operating a vending machine business are listed below.

In today's fast-paced world, vending machines have become a common sight. Vending machines exist in a variety of shapes and sizes, and they may be found almost anyplace. Vending machines can be found practically anywhere, including corporate buildings, schools, malls, and airports. As a result, the vending machine industry is one of the most profitable today. Many sellers will be glad to put your machines on their property because it is one of the simplest methods for them to make extra money with little work. However, there are a few things to consider before you get started with this business. The following are some prerequisites for operating a vending machine business:

A Specific Location

Finding a fantastic site is the first step in launching a successful vending machine business. A excellent location, such as a busy office building, a cafeteria, or even a large residential complex, should have a regular flow of clients. Laundromats and outdoor recreational spaces are examples of other ideal settings. For any vending machine business, a great location is essential.

Permits and Licenses for Businesses

You may need a company license or a vendor's license depending on where your vending machine business is located. You'll also need to find out if any federal or provincial organizations, such as the Department of Revenue or the Department of Motor Vehicles, require your firm to be registered. These criteria can differ from province to province and change on a regular basis, so make sure you check with any relevant local agencies for updates and make sure you have the appropriate permits.

Insurance

Your most crucial initial investment is liability insurance. Vending machine businesses have a reputation for being simple to start, but you still need insurance to protect your company and yourself from potential legal claims.

Customers want your machines to function properly when they use them. Customers can sue you if they receive food poisoning or other injuries as a result of an item you sold.

Work with an expert insurance agent to determine the appropriate level of coverage depending on the number of machines you expect to own and run, the places where they will be installed, and the products you will sell.

Finally, you must select what standards are appropriate for your vending machine business. Hopefully, the information we've provided has supplied you with the necessary information to make that decision.

Profits from Vending Machines

There isn't likely to be a single vending machine that makes life-changing money. A few strategically placed devices, on the other hand, can provide a steady stream of income. According to Brandongaille.com, the average person spends roughly $27 per year on vending machine products. In addition, the typical transaction costs $1.71.

A vending machine generates an average of $76 in revenue every week for the person who owns and operates it. This equates to more than $300 per month. As a result, you can see how a few machines producing an average can quickly turn a profit.

Vending machine spending in the United States Is still strong. The total amount spent each year exceeds $7 billion. Even so, the industry is still under pressure to provide healthier food and drink options. Some people may assume that such foods are less popular than junk food. However, sales of healthy snack foods outnumber those of junk food, according to statistics.

Vending Machines' Top 4 Profitable Machines
Sodas with a Name

Vending machines that dispense soda continue to be the most popular. And demand for cold drinks spikes in the summer. The machines look like the snack machines with glass fronts below. Specialty soda machines, on the other hand, are often delivered covered. Customers can choose from a wide range of drinks by pressing a button.

In addition, the machines are frequently branded with images and names of the popular soda brands that they sell.

Because the variety of drinks is considerably smaller than that of food, it is much easier for a vending machine franchise owner to keep their item selection small. There are a few umbrella firms that hold many soda brands, which are typically bundled together. For example, such machines are unlikely to stock both Pepsi and Coca-Cola. Cans, as well as 12oz and 20oz bottles, are available in various sizes.

Glass Front Snacks with Coil System

While the location of a vending machine has a lot to do with its profitability, there is no doubt that snack vending machines are one of the most popular. The most popular goods can vary by state, but there are many of examples that are popular almost everywhere.

Snickers, Twix, and Baby Ruth chocolate bars, as well as Doritos, Cheetos, and Lays chips, are all mainstays of these machines. Rice Crispy Treats, Grandma's Cookies, Granola Bars, Beef Jerky, and Pretzels are some of the other popular treats in these machines.

Because this type of machine has a glass front, the products can act as their own advertisement, eliminating the need to brand the machine. The dealer can readily adjust the things for sale as a result of this. The snacks are placed in a single or double coil system that rotates on its axis to transport each item along a single path when a client selects it, with the one in front dropping down into the collection area.

Food that has been refrigerated in the style of a turret

Cold foods such as salads, sandwiches, and burritos, as well as breakfast items and even whole meals, can be sold in refrigerated vending machines. Many of the foods in these machines will be ready to eat or require reheating, and frozen food will often be available as well.

This strategy of providing some cold and some frozen food allows customers to buy fresh food (which is more popular), but the vendor does not have to invest as much in things with a limited shelf life. There are still frozen products to sell if the fresh food runs out.

The turret-style vending machines have an internal display unit that can be turned by the consumer to see all of the offered items. This type of machine works well with cold food products since it gives the consumer a more personalized experience when they choose their meal.

Freestanding ice

The location of an ice vending machine is crucial to its success. It must be in a high-traffic area, such as adjacent to a convenience store or a petrol station, and once you've found a suitable place, the rest is rather simple.

There's no need to worry about which products will sell better than others; ice has no expiration date, and many people buy it in quantity for parties and vacations, or simply to fill up a cooler with it for home usage. Summer is undoubtedly the busiest season, but ice is in high demand all year.

Despite the necessity for regular refrigeration, maintaining an ice vending machine is not prohibitively expensive. Obviously, utility prices vary by location, but a reasonable estimate for water and electricity costs is $0.25 per 100 pounds of ice. Obviously, you'll need to do a lot more study before deciding whether ice is the ideal vending product for you. The cost of such equipment can vary substantially, while buying used may be an option to save money at first.

Chapter 7

Sales techniques that work in the vending machine business

Are you ready to open your own vending machine company? One thing you're probably already aware of is that, at least at first, you'll be a one-man show. Regardless matter how many machines you have, you'll be in charge of everything at first, from picking the types of machines you want to buy/lease to getting fantastic locations for them to negotiating a decent price with your vending stock suppliers.

Owning a business necessitates a working knowledge of a variety of topics, including sales and marketing, bookkeeping, operations, inventory management, and partner relations. Even if your company expands to the point where you have specialized route drivers, accountants, and inventory personnel, you'll still be the strategic thinker and chief negotiator when it comes to signing new contracts or extending old ones.

Naturally, none of us has the time to become an expert in every field, so we could all use some solid advice and direction on what industry best practices are and how they might be applied to our situation.

Because having the correct sales attitude and skillset is so important in beginning and maintaining a vending machine business, we thought we'd provide a few pointers on what to do and how to act when you need to put on your salesman's hat.

Before you initiate the first contact with a vending location owner/manager

Going into this first meeting prepared will give you a lot more confidence, make you better prepared to answer inquiries, and make you look more professional in your opponent's eyes.

a) Begin by determining what your value proposition is.

Consider what problem your service solves for the location manager. How is he better off now that my machines are stationed nearby? While end-customers, or actual buyers, drive your sales turnover, your target persona in this situation is the location manager; he's the gatekeeper who controls your access to consumers. Your offer should be able to help them improve their existing circumstances. Keep in mind, though, that you are not operating in a vacuum. Do you know if there are any more vending machines at the location? What services do they provide? What makes your offering better or unique? Your value proposition should be focused on what you can do for the location owner that is better than what the competition presently offers. It could be the range of snacks/sodas you offer, the payment methods you offer, or simply the fact that you respond faster and better to the demands of your POC. The location manager must value your value proposition, and it must be difficult for the competitors to duplicate.

b) Draw attention to the before/after contrast.

You should be able to present a strong story that builds on and enhances the status quo to help the location manager comprehend the added value your solution delivers to their site. Your goal is to make the distinction between today and when your machines are installed in their location in the future evident to your potential location manager. "Make the cost real, tangible, and terrible by amplifying the agony. How do you go about doing this?

How do you apply these questions to a location manager's negotiation? Make sure to ask questions that will assist you uncover the problem your prospect is currently facing so you can offer your service as a solution.

Analyze and manage your behavior

Analyze and control your conduct to take control of the conversation and boost your chances of a positive outcome from a meeting with the location manager (especially the first one).

Choose your initial statement carefully. Do not begin a meeting by complaining about the traffic/weather or how busy and weary you are. It simply sets the tone for the rest of the talk.

If a competitor has already moved in his equipment at the spot you're seeking to get, don't mention anything negative about them. Not only does gossip breed distrust and erode your trustworthiness, but it's also possible that your location manager will unconsciously and subconsciously associate those unfavorable characteristics with you. According to the Science of People, if you imply your competition is low-quality and untrustworthy, your potential client will automatically identify such characteristics with you.

Show that you have high expectations of your potential location manager — contrary to popular belief, using superlatives to characterize the person with whom you're conducting business, the location itself, end-customers, and so on actually works in your advantage. How? According to a survey, people generally live up to their favorable labels. "It's nice that we can have an open and honest chat," you can remark, or "You're such a pleasure to work with."

Keep an eye on your body language. According to research, salesmen who use nonverbal communication effectively are far more successful.

The summit should come to a close on a high note.

Details are being worked out.

Negotiating the details

Negotiation isn't something that can be learned in a day or two. There has been a great deal written and said about it, and there are hundreds, if not thousands, of courses and instructional materials available on the subject. However, one should not be intimidated or overwhelmed. While you can't expect to become a master negotiator after reading a few books, there are certain easy yet effective tactics you may use to help your prospect site manager and yourself create a win-win situation.

Be prepared to respond to any objections the property owner may have to your offer. You can't read people's minds, but if you try to put yourself in their shoes, you'll be able to come up with at least one or two misgivings. Before your prospect has even managed to articulate them, try to dissolve them (once said aloud, objections tend to solidify and gain ground).

Ask your opponent a lot of questions to get a clearer image of his current condition and to understand his pain areas so that you can address them later with your offer; being proactive allows you to control the pace and set of the conversation.

Make sure you get something in return if you agree to the location manager's demands. You shouldn't agree to all of the prospect's demands without also making some of your own. You build the foundation for a long-term, mutually beneficial relationship with your location manager by generating a win-win situation. If you agree to the commission they're asking for, for example, try to get a guarantee for the daily foot traffic that will pass by your machines.

Make sure you know the industry norm - if you've done your study, you should know what's customary for this location in terms of commission payable, machine servicing and presentation, the variety of merchandise that needs to be offered, and so on before approaching your location manager's office. Being prepared not only makes a good first impression on your opponent, but it also allows you to properly design your offer without losing money. Always begin with a slightly higher offer as a rule of thumb. Rather than agreeing to a high commission that isn't sustainable in the long run, try to add value.

Completing the transaction

It's always nerve-wracking to reach the last stages of a negotiation. There's always a chance you'll lose to the competition, they'll decide to postpone their decision, or they'll ask for a commission you can't support in the long run, no matter how happy you feel about your presentation thus far and how thrilled the prospect location manager is. However, using the appropriate words can make a difference: As you've already noticed, acting as if the prospect has already accepted your offer can come across as aggressive and drive them away: "When should I begin placing the machines in your venue?

Instead, make the location manager feel at ease without entirely removing the pressure:

Blunders made by a new vending machine operator

The last thing you want to do when starting a new business is make mistakes that could jeopardize your future success. It is preferable to learn from those who have gone before you and failed. Keep an eye on the coffee vending machine sector around the world and study their statistics to learn how to run a profitable business. The ten faults that new vending enterprises make should be avoided. They may not cover all of the potential dangers and issues that can occur in this type of business, but we hope they will aid you in your quest for a prosperous future.

1. Inaccurately calculating payback

One of the most typical blunders in any industry is predicting future profits that are larger than those that are realistically achievable. Vending machine supply providers usually claim that the cost of each machine will be repaid in less than a year. This is overconfident, and it may lead to new business owners taking on more than they can handle. While payback durations could be even shorter than the promised six months, there are so many variables and potential difficulties that it is difficult to anticipate the outcome. In actuality, most vending machines recoup their investment in 12 to 14 months through concession revenues.

2. Choosing Machine Models That Are Older and Simpler

Vending machines must compete for the attention and money of customers with a plethora of other options. Every machine you put in place must function properly, but that isn't enough to make a good profit. Your machines must emanate quality and security in order to succeed in the marketplace. While most vending machines endure 12 to 24 years, if they are not properly maintained, they may appear older than they should.

3. Installing Non-Working Pay Systems and Bill Validators

Not only could you miss out on some payments for things purchased from a malfunctioning vending machine, but purchasers will stop purchasing if their money isn't working. This can happen if customers pay but no product is delivered, or if the machine refuses to accept the coins or dollars they have.

4. Using Vending Machines on Credit or Lease

While investing in a new vending business is vital, newcomers may err on the side of doing too much, too fast. Realistic optimism must be balanced with optimism. If the sales don't come, using credit, taking out loans, or signing up for an extended lease arrangement can generate problems. Any gains you create may be eaten away by debt or loan payments.

5. Purchasing Machines in Large Quantities

While reductions on bulk vending machine purchases may appear appealing and may save you money in the long term, you must consider how many you can successfully deploy, set up, and service. People who are fresh to the vending industry may overestimate their talents. This may necessitate storing the machines unused for a period of time before finding a suitable location for them.

6. Installing Vending Machines in Inappropriate Locations

The most important factor in making money with a vending machine is its position. Of course, you'll need a visually appealing display front, high-quality products at reasonable pricing, and a quick turnaround time, but if the machine is located incorrectly, no one will ever buy. A terrible location is one where there is little foot traffic and other businesses' machines compete for their attention. Cafes, diners, and restaurants, among other food service establishments, can eat into your revenues. Another item to keep an eye on is the folks who would exploit it's peace of mind. People will be hesitant to stop at vending machines in dimly lit places.

7. Ignoring Local Consumers' Purchasing Habits or Capabilities

Know who your customers are and what they want. People in low-income neighborhoods may gladly spend 50 cents on a little snack yet balk at a $1 option.

8. Selling products or ingredients that are of poor quality or include defects

Consumers prefer trusted name-brand snacks to less expensive generic alternatives. Coffee is dependent not only on the grounds used, but also on the water quality. To make a tasty brew or snack, all of the elements must function together.

9. Failure to properly maintain, clean, and service machines on a regular basis

Consumer trust and willingness to buy are essential to any vending machine business. A soiled or defective equipment does not inspire confidence, and sales will suffer as a result.

10. Using Vending Machines That Appear to Be Old or Inactive

Older devices are not only more prone to break or go out of service, but they also don't create the impression of a strong, thriving organization. Older models with dull, unappealing graphics perform worse than newer models.

Chapter 8
Tips on How to Grow Your Vending Machine Business

For most entrepreneurs, each venture is a chance. With little work, you can amass a large sum of money or lose it. That is not to say, however, that entrepreneurs cannot invest in vending machines. You can significantly enhance vending machine earnings by following these six strategies.

Perhaps you're interested in learning how to start your own vending machine business from the experts at Allied Vending. Perhaps you're dissatisfied with your present salary or wish to increase it. If this applies to you, you may want to explore starting a vending machine business.

Choose the Product You Wish to Sell

Vending machines can be sold in a variety of ways. The majority of people connect vending machines with the candy and beverage machines that are typically located outside supermarkets. Vending machines, on the other hand, can be used to sell items such as candy, gum, and stickers.

Vending machines that are refrigerated are ideal for snacks and lunch. Vending machines rent and sell toiletries, as well as personal things. Electronic vending machines selling charges and wireless headphones are available in airports. Consider the things you wish to offer before calculating the startup costs.

Locate Your Product Appropriately

As is the case with any retail business, a vending machine's location is critical to its success. The most advantageous sites are those that provide the greatest variety of opportunities. The locations of your businesses should correspond to the things that you sell. Vending machines are not appropriate at a good location. However, you're likely to discover that the most desirable places in your neighborhood are already taken. The goods you choose should be appropriate for the location and traffic volume in which they will be used. Even the most popular products may fail to sell in a congested region if the target market is the wrong one.

Establish a Market Focus

Any company plan must include market research. This is also applicable to this industry. You're almost certain to have come across vending machines selling snacks or beverages while out and about. In churches, schools, entertainment centers, and other places where people congregate, they may require food in between meals. Vending machines are useful for folks in these settings who require a quick snack or beverage. Perhaps you were unaware of how well-kept vending machines are. Even small and medium-sized firms can contribute in this manner to their communities.

Summary

If you have vending and business experience, starting your own vending firm may make sense. You'll need to locate reliable vending machine companies, acquire training, and pick the finest vending sites for your business. This can take significantly longer if you have never worked in vending before. As a result, setting up a vending machine business can be challenging and time-consuming for a novice. Starting your own vending machine business is ideal for people who are confident in their ability to negotiate the best deals and are willing to invest a significant amount of time in the business's development.

Trends in Vending Machines to Be Aware Of

This year has been a year of winds of change, and it would be naive to believe that they will have no effect on vending machine trends in the coming years. With the advancement of smart technology and the changing needs of consumers, you can say goodbye to old, rusty vending machines that take your money and then stop working. They can now serve you with a single click on your smartphone, in addition to offering varied food and beverage alternatives.

The vending machine industry is booming and diversifying beyond traditional food and beverage retailing. Vending machines have evolved to contain gadgets, electronics, and other essential equipment. The sector is expected to grow to 5426.9 million USD in value by 2023 as horizons broaden. Are you able to envision the revenue potential?

This is an industry that has been neglected on every level: from technology and product range to user experience and industry operators, there is so much that can be improved. Today, we're going to reveal seven vending machine trends that will shape the industry for the foreseeable future.

1. Cashless transactions

Carrying cash all of the time and having the correct quantity of coins is inconvenient, which is why more and more individuals are opting for debit and credit cards, as well as mobile payments. From 2014 to 2017, the number of card payments per person in Lithuania more than doubled, and the figure continues to rise. Not to mention the fact that more individuals are paying for goods and services using their cellphones.

Vending machines have only accepted coins and bills for a long time, but cashless payments are about to change that. You can now swipe your credit card and have the payment accepted by a machine. Modern vending machines can also be accessed via mobile apps that can not only process payments but also show what's in stock and provide more targeted offers based on your previous purchases. Personalization will be discussed later in this text.

For the time being, let's just remember that no firm can survive in today's market without the capacity to accept cashless payments. It's a company driver, a must-have, and a business pillar. The world is rapidly moving away from cash, and the vending machine sector must adapt.

2. Payment protection

The second development in the vending machine industry is greater payment security, which is driven by the possibility of cashless payment. Although swiping your card satisfies everyone's desire for speed and convenience, it isn't always the safest option. Due to data breaches and scams, the vending industry is collaborating with financial institutions to maintain the highest level of security.

European citizens can rest easy because the European Union passed PSD2 in 2019. (Payment Service Directive). Strong Customer Authentication (SCA) is ensured by the directive, which protects your data and bank accounts from breaches and illicit money withdrawals.

Vending machine operators will benefit from increased transparency and security as a result of the new rule. If you make a large payment, however, a machine may require an additional authentication procedure. In this area, there is still potential for improvement, but payment security is a slow-burning fire that requires time and thorough preparation to accomplish its desired outcome.

3. Shops that are fully automated

Amazon has been experimenting with automated retail for some time. Amazon Go, the company's first automated store, opened in 2016, and it was a watershed moment for unattended shopping. Despite the fact that vending machines are normally fully automated, this could be the start of something bigger.

As the industry expands, so will industry trends, which will include a greater range of commodities such as food, soft drinks, hot beverages, and other items normally seen in supermarkets. Additionally, voice commands may improve the service by making it more intelligible and accessible to all users.

The amount of automation can be greatly improved, bringing the entire industry closer to the digital standards that consumers expect. You don't need studies to prove that people are accustomed to some amount of automation in all aspects of their lives. Manual participation has diminished dramatically, and the vending machine business is projected to follow suit.

4. Vending machines: It's time for more variety.

We can now put technology aside and return to the heart of the vending machine industry: the commodities inside the machines. You usually picture an ancient box loaded with chips, a drink, or some nibbles when you think about vending machines. This is no longer the case.

To satisfy shifting consumer expectations, retailers began focusing on broader food alternatives and even devices. Vending machines of the future offer a variety of healthy food options, including vegan and gluten-free options. Customers searching for an energy boost or a quick snack have options as well.

Consumers now expect to see umbrellas, headphones, and other comparable goods in terms of product variety. Many shops still resist putting more expensive items in vending machines, although these industry habits are shifting as safety and vandalism rates improve.

The vending machine business is expanding, and it is no longer limited to packaged foods, as is becoming clear. Vending machines are now pushing less junk food, better options, and a shift toward healthy eating in general.

The variety of products offered by new vending machines isn't the only thing that makes them unique. According to studies, the number of vending machines on the market will grow, as will the number of sites where they may be found. Vending machine sales will rise in the next years, from eateries and local convenience stores to apartment communities, hotels, schools, aircraft, trains, manufacturing sites, and office buildings.

5. Environmentally friendly options

Nobody should be proud of this statistic: in 2016, 5 tons of rubbish were produced per European resident, with just 37% of that being recycled. This adds up to millions of tons of waste produced annually around the world, and because only a small portion of it is recycled, retailers must act.

As a response, vending machine manufacturers are developing reverse vending machines that recycle packaging once the product has been consumed. One of the most essential innovations and steps toward combining business and the health and well-being of our planet is this ability. We have a responsibility to protect the environment, and any modern corporation worth its salt should remember this.

Companies such as Coca-Cola, Tesco, and Co-Op created their own versions of this solution, altering market dynamics as well as future trends, and speeding up vending machine production of comparable standard. You realize how important it is when you see industry leaders heading in that way.

6. Field management software is required for vending machine operators.

We may talk about automated vending machines all we want, but nothing happens unless teams are in charge of the upkeep. Vending machine owners realize the importance of vending machine operators and how even the little inconvenience can cause them to miss work.

Many of these challenges arise as a result of inadequate employee scheduling and dispatching. It prompted businesses to invest in digital technologies to aid in the planning of vending operations. Vending field service management software is a great tool for managing your employees, planning routes, and assigning jobs. Furthermore, you will have access to reporting, a calendar, and communication channels.

A strong field service management software can be the differentiator in the vending market, allowing your company to stand out. It's the tool that your customers never see, an internal solution that improves your operators' performance and eliminates all of the operational issues you've been dealing with up to this point.

7. Vending machines that are interactive, personalized, and smart

Vending machines, like everything else in our lives, will reach a stage where they build their own algorithm. Although vending machine technology may not yet be at that level, don't be shocked if this occurs in the near future. What exactly are we discussing?

You take out your phone, open the vending machine app, and sign into your account. The rest of the process is simple: you select multiple products from the machine, check out using the app, and then just retrieve the items from the machine.

The benefit of this entire process is that it provides for a personalized user experience. The app remembers your preferences, so the next time you log in, you'll get things like recommendations and notifications for new vending machine items.

With this new type of technology, the possibilities are infinite, since the app may lead you to the nearest vending machine or notify you if one is out of service. Consumers' interactions with vending machines become more engaged, dynamic, and results-oriented almost instantly.

Recap of the vending machine industry

For a long time, the modest vending machine has been disregarded and dismissed as an industry. The truth is that the more knowledge you get about the sector, the more you recognize its potential and new business opportunities.

Chapter 9
Types of Vending Machines for Your Business

Vending machines are a great way for your business to improve the client experience while also earning cash. They give an unattended resource for client satisfaction and offer more possibilities than you might believe.

Do you want to put vending machines in your business? Let's have a look at the different vending machines to see which one would be best for you.

Vending Machines for Food and Drink

Bulk vending machines with a variety of food and drink options are a terrific way to provide consumers with meal alternatives without having to invest in a kitchen. Here are a few samples of the various varieties that are available:

Vending Machines for Soft Drinks

When people hear the word vending machine, the first thing that comes to mind is soft drinks. Some machines sell bottled water as an alternative to soft beverages. Some of the water kinds available in these machines are seltzer or sparkling water, vitamin water, and flavored water. It's critical to offer a variety of options due to shifting customer habits when it comes to sugary drinks.

Vending Machines for Snacks

Candy bars, chips, and chocolates are all popular snack foods. There are other machines that specialize in one type of snack (e.g., cookie and chip machines).

Snack Vending Machines

Snacks are ideal for pick-up and go situations. Snack combo vending machines, on the other hand, are vending machines that may offer a variety of different snacks.

Vending Machines for Coffee

Coffee and tea are still very popular, so having a variety is crucial. Self-service workplaces, such as offices and conference rooms, as well as business-to-customer services, such as petrol stations, are growing more common.

Vending Machines with Cooked and Frozen Food

These gadgets are excellent for event planning. Perhaps you host a variety of outdoor and indoor events, such as weddings, conferences, sporting events, or birthday celebrations. In that instance, serving freshly prepared or ice-cold food and beverages is a great approach to keep your clients satisfied.

At sporting events, hot food vending machines such as hot dogs, burgers, and fries are popular. In contrast, ice cream vending machines, especially for outdoor visitor attractions, keep visitors calm while they roam around your facility and have a good time.

Vending Machines with Multiple Functions

These are a popular all-in-one solution for any work on a budget because they allow you to do a variety of things with only one machine. They're ideal if you want to provide a variety of snacks or drinks but don't want to spend a lot of money on them individually.

These vending machines are ideal for regions with a lot of foot activity. They offer a variety of snacks and beverages to their customers. You won't have to buy many machines for different items, and you'll be able to put together combinations that meet everyone's requirements.

Reception areas and corridors, as well as canteens in larger businesses, are high-traffic areas that create fantastic settings.

Vending Machines of Other Types

It's important to note that not all vending machines sell food or beverages. Here are some extra possibilities that you might not have considered at first:

Merchandiser

This style is most commonly used by hoteliers to provide toiletries to their guests. They are, nevertheless, useful in vending supplies such as

COVID-19 kits in some large industrial or office contexts. Toilet paper, tissues, pens and pencils, and even copier cartridges are examples.

Business cards, pens, pencils, and even staplers can be found in them in many office settings. They're useful if your employees are continually running out of or in need of these items.

Despite the fact that most firms provide an infinite supply of such products to their employees, these machines are more commonly encountered in communal workspaces. A media hub, for example, is a place where freelancers operate in an open-plan office environment.

Vending Machines in the Park

Outdoor vending machines provide food and beverages in the open air, making them an excellent addition to parks, gardens, and outdoor workplace areas.

Not only can outdoor versions of food and drink machines exist, but they can also be used to sell outdoor merchandise. They may also assist with emergency supplies if you run camps, activity businesses, or a leisure center that needs towels and energy supplements.

Vending Machines with Intelligence

Some of the most common use cases are contactless payment and collection. For anyone operating in an environment where contamination of any kind is common, not touching the machine is really beneficial. A laboratory or a food factory are two examples. Some machines even have smartphone apps that allow you to reserve and pay for items.

Vending Machines with a Personal Touch

People have personalized vending machines since the first one was invented in Greece over 2000 years ago. The most popular option is to use your decals and images to brand an existing vending machine model.

Vending machine images can be customized to match your company's branding needs.

Vending Machines with a Twist

These are ideal for use in waiting rooms or other areas where a large number of people are present, such as a medical clinic. They're also great for places where there are large lines and wait times.

A novelty vending machine can also be an excellent product launch marketing approach. You can modify the exterior and add your new product, or if your launch product is too huge or you have a significant budget, you can always sell your branded goods for free.

The Internet of Things (IoT) Has Changed Vending Machines in 8 Ways

When three graduate students and an engineer at Carnegie Mellon University devised a foolproof method of getting a cold Coke from the department's drink vending machine in 1982, no one realized they were creating the first example of what would later be known as the Internet of Things (IoT).

To communicate whether the machine had Coke in stock, the first intelligent vending machine used the ARPANET, a primitive version of the internet. On the machine's side, it kept track of the indicator lights that flashed when someone bought a Coke and stayed lighted when the machine was empty.

Anyone with an ARPANET connection could check the status of those lights and see if they could get a cold Coke. The concept gained a lot of traction among thirsty graduate students who didn't want to walk all the way to the machines just to find them empty or with warm beverages.

The system remained operational for years, but when Coke's bottle design evolved, the machine became obsolete. For the next 30 years, hardly one thought about it again, until individuals started integrating internet connectivity into industrial and daily products.

Now that the world is filled with billions of "connected things," vending machines and IoT technologies have combined once more. The internet-connected vending machine's usefulness has advanced far beyond what a group of thirsty grad students could have imagined.

1. Inventory management that is smart

IoT usually begins where it can have the greatest impact, and intelligent vending was no exception. Grad students required caffeine and sugar, so they devised a system for monitoring soft drink availability from their desks.

Years later, as the Internet of Things (IoT) took off and commerce began to look at vending machines and IoT technologies on a larger scale, this feature aided manufacturer and distributor adoption. Novotech, VendSoft, VendMAX, Supply Wizards, and other linked vending machine partners use smart tracking technology to maintain customers' favorites in stock without over-delivering items.

Distributors can also use IoT technology to keep track of stock in particular machines, ensuring that the product mix matches what customer's desire.

• Collect usage data to optimize resupply

- track contributing sales aspects, such as time of year, geography, and more, using sensor data and built-in analytics
- Make more precise resupply plans by forecasting sales.
- Track refill shipments
- Prioritize restocking to more profitable equipment

One worldwide food and beverage firm realized a 15% decrease in supply chain expenses and a 5% boost in revenue in a single division by incorporating IoT technology into its network of vending machines

2. Reduced theft and downtime

This technology is expected to lower the cost of theft by 5% for the food and beverage industry mentioned above. Vending machine theft, as well as mechanical failure and vandalism, can drastically diminish their profitability. IoT technology can lessen the occurrence and impact of these losses by tracking the performance and structural integrity of machines. If the program detects a potential problem or theft pattern, it might send out an alert for vending machine maintenance.

3. Energy efficiency

Intelligent vending can also save money by lowering the amount of energy required to cool products, all while maintaining a positive customer experience. When no one is there, occupancy sensors switch off the display and turn off the active cooling for a machine in a climate-controlled room. To keep the product cool, these sensors can turn the machine back on when someone enters the room or at predetermined intervals.

4. Content marketing at the point of sale

Customers would pay a snack vending machine some pennies or a banknote in the days before the Internet of Things, and it would give them a candy bar. Today, anyone can stroll up to a vending machine and obtain the latest entertainment news, a promotional offer, or even play a game.

Consumers and brands that operate internet-connected vending machines will have more engaging interactions as a result of these interactive content experiences. Companies can even alter up their content in reaction to client feedback or synchronize content delivery with a new campaign, resulting in more meaningful customer interactions. Intelligent vending, when combined with the right strategy, can become one of the most responsive delivery channels in the marketing department's arsenal.

5. Customized shopping

According to Forbes magazine, "extreme customization" is the driving force behind marketing today. More than 90% of customers prefer to purchase with companies that tailor their experiences to them, and 74% value the capacity to construct dynamic profiles to support those experiences.

Merchants can provide tailored experiences that customers might not expect from a vending machine by merging vending machines with IoT technology. Customers of today's vending machines can register user accounts, save personal preferences, and receive personalized incentives and notifications based on their purchasing habits.

The Freestyle vending machines from Coca-Cola are a great example. Customers can make their own drinks using Coke products and flavored syrups in these machines, which are now found at movie theaters and fast-food restaurants around the country.

Without an account, anyone can use the Freestyle machines, but there is also the possibility to customize your experience. Customers may bookmark their favorite blends, view deals, and earn rewards by simply downloading the Freestyle app. A user might order a half-Coke, half-Dr. Pepper combination with a hint of strawberry taste with a single tap on their phone, among more than 100 other alternatives.

6. Marketing based on data

Coca-Cola set aside 16 million unique network identifiers for its Freestyle network in the early 2010s. Coke can use these identifiers to figure out what kinds of blends people are making, as well as where and when they're doing it. The corporation may use the information to not only refill its machines, but also to determine which blends to advertise and where.

Comparative A/B testing is conceivable for a corporation like Coke, or any other with a good intelligent vending arrangement. The data could advise the organization which merchandising arrangements, display designs, or pricing points lead to the greatest sales by comparing one setup choice to another, given similar customer profiles and conditions.

7. Vending machines that do not accept cash

Most folks today recall the typical vending machine payment issue. You'd put your money in, and the machine would return it to you, either because the paper was crumpled or because the scanner was malfunctioning.

Crumpled notes are a thing of the past thanks to sophisticated vending POS software. Companies like Nayax make it simple to pay using a variety of payment apps like Venmo, PayPal, Apple Pay, and Google Pay.

Four out of every five consumers in the United States use at least one of these apps. Millennials are the most likely to utilize payment applications, with 94 percent of them doing so. Even among baby boomers, who are the least inclined to employ cashless payment, payment applications are used by over two-thirds of them.

Customers can buy utilizing these apps thanks to built-in internet connections in today's vending machines. Customers won't have to worry about transporting cash to the vending machine because of this. This is significant, given that only 16% of customers still carry cash.

For two reasons, client convenience leads to increased sales:

- Customers can purchase at any time, not just when they have cash on hand.

- Customers consider the seller to be more relevant and aware of their demands.

8. Ordering without touching

Customers' requirements are met in a variety of ways by intelligent vending, including cashless payment. Coke adopted a contactless QR-based ordering mechanism to their network of Freestyle vending machines in the summer of 2020, when many people were terrified of touching shared, public surfaces owing to coronavirus. Customers can now order using their smartphones without ever touching a shared surface by scanning a QR code on the machine.

Because of its existing intelligent vending operating system, Coke was able to create this breakthrough fast. Thousands of Freestyle machines may start employing this new technology with just a few tweaks to the software code made from home.

You don't have to be Coca-Cola to add cutting-edge user-centric capabilities. With a connected vending system like Novotech's, you can create a network that adjusts to what your customers want and need from a vending machine.

Chapter 10

Vending Machine Business Pros & Cons

Vending machines provide a number of advantages that make starting a vending machine business appealing, especially to first-time entrepreneurs with low funds. However, there is a lot of self-serving sales information about vending machine profitability and what it takes to thrive — otherwise known as hokum. While there are numerous advantages to operating a vending machine business, there are also some disadvantages.

Low start-up costs are a plus.

A considerable sum of money is frequently required to pay the initial expenditures of starting a firm. However, with just a little cash, a vending machine business may be up and going in no time. In fact, you might start for as low as a few hundred dollars, which would cover the cost of a single secondhand machine. It's a terrific method to see if this business is right for you without having to invest a lot of money or quit your day job.

Pro: Starting small reduces the risk of failure.

Starting your company on a smaller scale also lowers your financial risk. You can get an idea of how much money you might be able to generate in the industry by starting with a single machine. You can learn about the ins and outs of running a vending business, such as stocking frequency, location, and marketing. You haven't lost a lot of money if you discover that the business isn't for you.

Pro: As the boss, you have a lot of flexibility.

You are the boss when you own a vending machine firm. You have complete control over your working hours and the regularity with which you service and replenish your machines. You can choose where you want your machines to go and make deals with the store owners. There is also a lot of schedule freedom because your machine is selling your stuff for you without you having to be physically present.

Controlling the growth of your company is a plus.

The success of your vending business may be determined by the things you sell, but the decision is ultimately yours. You can choose solutions that promise to be the most profitable for you based on market research and industry trends. Most operators advise vending things that cost a third of what they may sell for and generate as close to a $1 profit every transaction as possible.

Con: Profitability is scale-dependent.

If you stick to the small-scale method and a single machine, you could generate as little as $5 to $10 per week, which means you won't get far if your growth strategy is to just reinvest in the company. If you earn $25 per month, it will take you little under three years to save enough money from profits to purchase your second secondhand machine. While vending machine companies tout your ability to make a lot of money quickly, you shouldn't expect to make a lot of money right away.

Cons: It's not a hands-off business.

Your labor as a business owner does not finish once you've set up your machine and stocked it with merchandise. To maintain your success, you may need to shift machines from one site to another until you find one that is cost-effective. It's also possible that you'll need to change your product offerings. You may be ready to grow once you've found a formula that works, which involves more hours and footwork.

Con: There's a lot of competition for prime locations.

Another factor that might have a significant impact on your revenues is location competition. Blue-collar workers buy twice as much vending machine products as white-collar workers, hence areas with a higher number of blue-collar workers are the best. You also don't want to be in an area where vending machines are already aplenty, nor do you want to be the owner of a vending machine situated in an area where customers are rare.

Cons: Additional Costs to Consider

A desirable location may be sought after by your competitors, therefore obtaining one may need paying a fee to the site's owners. You'll have to pay for the space you take up and the electricity your machine consumes at any site. This is usually a pre-determined percentage of your earnings.

Cons: Long working hours

Owning a business may provide you more work freedom, but you'll almost certainly wind up working longer and harder than you would in a typical job. The more equipment you have, the more time you'll have to spend replenishing and maintaining them. To be successful, you must have a strong dedication, work long hours, and have consistent work habits.

Outside influences on decision-making are a disadvantage.

Another factor to consider when starting a vending machine business is the growing tendency away from sweet foods, which have traditionally been the mainstay of the industry. Sales of sweet snacks and sodas are increasingly being regulated, with merchants being compelled to pay additional taxes on these sales.

Consider these advices when selecting the best vending machine

Starting a vending machine company might be the best business idea you've ever had. You will, however, need to get the greatest pros to provide you with healthy you vending. This could be the most nerve-wracking part. You'll need to conduct extensive research on the greatest machine distributors. Here are some pointers to help you identify the best machine dealers from the numerous that may be in your area.

Take a look at the machine pricing. Make sure you visit at least three different machine dealers to evaluate and contrast prices. Consider the machine vendors with the most affordable prices. There's no reason to pay more when the same computer can be had for the same price. High pricing do not always imply high-quality goods or services.

Make sure you work with vendors who provide excellent customer service. Good customer service makes you feel at ease and encourages you to return for more of the same. It also gives the assurance that if something goes wrong, you can contact the supplier and that he or she will be happy to handle the problem without complaint.

Ensure that the machine provider provides you with adequate training until you are competent to use the machines. Healthy You Vending, for example, gives appropriate training to their customers to ensure that they have the necessary hands-on expertise to operate the machines. As a result, it is the finest vendor to work with because their training is free. They also provide their clients with any information that may be needed while using the machine.

Make sure you deal with merchants who are located all over the world. As a result, you can use their services without difficulty. Companies with an internet presence may be easier to work with because you can access their information even before seeing them in person. This reduces the amount of guessing involved in finding machine vendors.

It's also crucial to ensure that the machines are of excellent quality. The high quality of the machines allows you to have a wide range of options so you may change your menu and stay on top of things. Some devices keep meals warm overnight, allowing you to conserve energy that would otherwise be used to warm it the next day. To avoid annoyance in the future, always opt for high-quality devices.

Permit for Vending Machines and Devices

Adding a vending machine or two to your lobby or office might help you generate more cash with little effort. However, before you start making money, you must first obtain your vending machine/device permit. First, you need to get a vending machine license from your state. Then, you can put a vending machine on your property. If it takes money in exchange for food, drink, or anything else, it's a vending machine. It also needs a business license.

Assuring that your vending machine is clean

As part of your vending machine permit, you may also need to have your vending machine checked by the health department in your area.

Because food is involved, your local health department wants to make sure it fulfills specific safety standards and that the food in the machine hasn't expired.

If an inspection is required, contact your city's business licenses, permits, and tax board.

How to Get a Vending Machine Permit

To make it easier, gather all of the essential information before filing your application. Begin by doing the following:

• If your machine will sell beverages, you'll need a beverage license.

• Employer Identification Number (FEIN)

• Sales tax identification number

• If applicable, a food service license

• Make a plan for where you'll put the vending machine.

You will be contacted to schedule an opening inspection once you have completed the vending machine/device license application. The machine should be in the location where you intend to keep it at this stage so that the inspector can assess if the location and contents of the machine comply with the city's requirements.

What is your role as a vending machine owner?

It is your obligation to schedule the machine's stocking with a trustworthy vendor who will replace expired food with fresh goods, as well as to keep the machine clean at all times. For the same reasons, you, as the owner, should inspect it on a regular basis.

Make sure the machine is always operational, and that your contact information is stored on the machine in case of a problem. Pay your renewal costs before they expire to keep your license current.

Profits are served up by next-generation vending machines.

Vending machines are no longer limited to the sale of snacks and beverages. In a few of minutes, today's "next-generation" vending machines can provide fresh salads and hot pizza.

According to Technavio, the intelligent vending machine industry would expand by $9.33 billion by 2024, at a CAGR of over 22%.

Key market participants

Fresh salads are dispensed via Farmer's Fridge vending machines for healthful and convenient on-the-go solutions. Salad jars, as well as other nutritious meals and snacks, are dispensed by the automated smart fridges. According to The Wall Street Journal, the company has over 400 machines in office buildings, hospitals, and food courts across six states.

The internet-connected smart vending machines allow the corporation to monitor food safety from afar. Farmer's Fridge claims to make, deliver, and sell salads in 36 hours or less, and it won't sell a salad after 48 hours.

Chowbotics, which was acquired by DoorDash earlier this year, is another handy salad option. According to The Spoon, DoorDash is currently testing Chowbotics' Sally robot to make private label salads and microwaveable meals for sale at its DashMart delivery-only convenience stores (July 30). In under 90 seconds, the salad-making robot combines up to eight ingredients in a disposable bowl.

Meanwhile, Basil Street is introducing self-serve pizza ovens. The 22-square-foot units make flash-frozen 10-inch pizzas in roughly three minutes at the push of a button, according to Meat + Poultry (Aug. 4).

"Globally, automated food kiosks are recognized as a viable option for on-the-go meals," CEO Delgin Kenealy told Meat + Poultry. "As a result of the epidemic, the demand for contact-free solutions is increasing in the United States."

According to Vending Market Watch, Vancouver-based Up Meals recently launched out a smart vending machine solution at Simon Fraser University for students (June 8). According to the business, the machine will provide students with 24/7 access to healthy, sustainable meal alternatives, and the menu will be curated based on a survey given to groups of students to determine the types of cuisine they want to see.

WHERE DOES INTEREST COME FROM?

Though some smart vending machines existed prior to 2020, the COVID-19 epidemic has accelerated their development.

Carla Balakgie, CEO of the National Automatic Merchandising Association, claimed in a Washington Post piece that pandemic fears and social alienation had boosted vending machine adoption. She told the publication, "It's touch less, it's considered safe, and it's prepared so things haven't been fondled or breathed on."

Meanwhile, Kenealy of Basil Street told Vending Times that the pandemic boosted demand for the machines across the United States. "Because our process minimizes touchpoints, decision-makers within these locations have identified our Automated Pizza Kitchens (APK) as a wonderful option," he explained.

"People are realizing that a high-volume, retail food solution like our APK can feed a lot of people with a lot less danger of food- or human-borne illness," he added.

4 Things to Know About Vending Machine Card Readers

If you're always on the move and don't want to wait in line for snacks or beverages, or if you're at work and need a caffeine boost, chances are you've stopped by a vending machine. They're quick and easy to use, and they don't require any human interaction.

Aside from the occasional discomfort of trying to shake your bag of pretzels free from the vendor's last rung when it becomes stuck, the machine is likely to be very stress-free. But what if the machine doesn't give you your change or, worse still, refuses to accept your crumpled bills?

Chip card reading technology is being installed in newer vending machines, and it's crucial to keep up with the changes.

1. To use a vending machine, you don't need a chip-enabled card...yet.

At the very least, not yet. Vending machines still include a stripe to swipe your card, a slot for cash and coins, and some have been modified to accommodate chip readers because banks are currently transitioning from magnetic stripe to chip reader cards.

Dip your card in vending machines the same way you would at a store's checkout counter. The screen will ask you to insert your card, interact with your bank, verify your transaction, and then ask you to remove your card.

One thing to keep in mind is that there is no one working at a vending machine to remind you to dip. Right present, all cards with chips also include the magnetic stripe, but it doesn't imply you have the option to use it. The magnetic stripe reader in the vending machine is for people who have yet to receive a chip-enabled card. If you try to swipe your card and it refuses to allow you proceed with the purchase, it's most likely because it recognizes that your card contains a chip and is waiting for you to dip it.

2. Just because it's unattended, security doesn't take a back seat.

Payments made at vending machines will not be any less secure than payments made at a payment terminal manned by a person, according to the people who design payment terminals. It's just as safe to put your card in a vending machine as it is to put it in the attachment on a cashier's tablet.

The process of encrypting your purchase occurs inside the hardware where you enter your card. Whatever snack or drink you purchased has a data code that is unique to your card and your purchase, just like everything else. Chip-reading technology is so fraud-resistant because it changes every time you make a purchase in that vending machine.

Your transaction code is provided to your bank, which then transfers it to the receiving bank, completing your purchase. You won't be asked for a PIN number or a signature when using a vending machine.

Keep in mind that chip transactions take a fraction of a second longer than magnetic stripe transactions. This is due to the fact that payment information is transmitted in real time and must be encrypted. When your payment is secure and you don't have to worry about fraud over something as basic as a two-dollar beverage or a 75-cent bag of M&M's, a few extra seconds spent at the vending machine is well worth it.

3. Contactless Payments Could Be a Possibility

Because many businesses are adopting payment systems like Apple Pay, Google Pay, and others, vending machine card reader technology must evolve to keep up.

Consider the last time you went to the mall and had a strong desire for an ice-cold Coke. Although it used to be as simple as removing a buck from your pocket and waiting for the bottle to fall, there are now three options for paying for a drink like this: digital wallet, cash, or credit card.

You never know who's carrying what these days. Some people prefer to pay with cash. Some people choose to make larger credit payments and smaller cash payments. Some people don't want to deal with either and have saved their credit card information to a digital wallet.

If you prefer a digital wallet, it may be difficult to find a vending machine that exclusively accepts frictionless payment choices for the time being. Instead, some vending machine owners replace the payment terminal with a different one and preserve the unit. This short upgrade implies that the vending machine card reader will still take cash and magnetic stripe technology, but chip scanners will now be able to use them as well.

Just because chip credit cards have Near Field Communication (NFC) capabilities doesn't mean this payment method is accepted by all vending machines. Some vending machine card readers lack the essential technology to process contactless payments. You'll have to search the terminal for the symbol. A circle with radiofrequency lines and a hand holding a card indicates that the payment terminal will accept a digital wallet payment.

4. Get to Know Your Clientele

When it comes to modernizing your vending machines, including cashless choices might not be a terrible idea. Is it, however, cost-effective?

While many individuals are still hesitant to use credit cards for modest purchases, it's nevertheless convenient to have the choice if they forget to take cash out or leave their wallet at home before going to the vending machine. Because credit card spending has become more common in recent years due to its ease of use, adding the option to your vending machine may increase sales. Customers are increasingly opting for time-saving choices. They also feel considerably more at ease while using credit cards because EMV goes to such lengths to keep personal information secure and protected.

If your vending machine attracts people of various generations, it's likely that they'll want to pay in a variety of methods. If your vending machines are in workplaces where most customers are familiar with them and know they only accept cash, it may not be worth the cost of replacing them with vending machine card readers. If your vending machine is in an area with a lot of young professionals who rarely carry cash, a refit might be a good idea.

Select the Best Design

When it comes to updating your vending machine with new payment terminals, keep it simple. You don't want a vending machine card reader to intimidate your customers. It should be as uncomplicated as possible. Vending machines, after all, are all about convenience.

Customers will be more trusting of how safe a kiosk or vending machine is if it appears to be simple to operate. This is because it won't be difficult for them to figure out where the card goes and whether they should leave it in or pull it out before the transaction is complete.

Made in the USA
Monee, IL
06 September 2022